LYDIA LUNCH THE GUN IS LOADED

black dog publishing
london uk

CONTENTS

ROTTEN INCANDESCENCE

*"There is no one who can kiss
without feeling the smile of those without faces;
there is no one who can touch
an infant and forget the immobile skulls of horses."*

Federico García Lorca

There is little simple catharsis in Lydia Lunch's work.
Any emotional expulsion is visceral rather than
psychological; this is vermiculation and abjection
rather than simple abreaction. There is little desire
to entertain, to sate the demands of the audience.
This is not to say that pleasure does not exist in
this work, but the events and emotional exchanges
experienced as pleasure may be unrecognisable
to many who flee the very desire and urges that
motivate and drive Lunch ever downward into
the quagmire.

Beginning in 1976 the teenage runaway squatted
downtown New York, stayed in Kitty Bruce's
apartment, and hung out at CBGBs and a handful of
other haunts of the emerging punk scene. But when
punk began to bloat, No Wave was ready to erase
its cadaver. Spewing simple atavistic brutality rooted
in noise minimalism, free jazz, and the possibility of
violence, No Wave was a response to the oedipal
whine of punks killing their fathers in order to
replace them. No Wave sought a ferocity that spoke
most often of the futility and hopelessness not just
of current existence but of the very nature of all
possible existence.

Lunch's primary contribution to No Wave was as
vocalist and guitarist of Teenage Jesus and The
Jerks, whose scant recorded output and short life
belies their ongoing influence on both experimental
and rock music. Characterised by jarring and
punctuating drum beats and howling distorted
slide guitar, the music was constructed as an aural
assault which punctuated Lunch's vocalisation. Her
subsequent musical explorations have not seen this
sonic intensity diminished, even if No Wave in its
purist manifestation was by necessity short lived.
No Wave remains central, the rigorous ferocity
and beauty that defined it informs all of Lunch's

subsequent creative practice. Simply put: experiment with the medium, push the boundaries, confront the self and the audience, remain authentic to the creative vision, regret nothing, do not debase individual creativity. Her work across film, theatre, spoken word, literature and fine art maintains these lessons, and continues to plough a series of themes that trace an economy of despair, and delineate an esotopia of willing psycho-sexual annihilation.

"I OPEN MYSELF TO MY ABSENCE."

What Is Memory (Lydia Lunch, *Shotgun Wedding*)

"I'M STARING INTO NOWHERE."

Stares To Nowhere (Lydia Lunch, *1313*)

"I FOUND SOMEPLACE IN LIMBO I'M TRYING TO CRAWL OUT OF, I'M TRYING TO CRAWL OUT OF, I'M TRYING TO CRAWL IN."

Twisted (Lydia Lunch)

Lunch's work recognises and celebrates unleashed desire and libidinal irruption. The urge for sexual discourse may be a dull commonplace of glossy tabloid magazines and daytime television but within dominant narratives sex is often rudimentarily presented simply as a source of trouble, a problem in need of a solution, or veiled behind a closed 'politically correct' narrative. In Lunch's work sexual desire becomes a subject that is explored with the exceptional clarity of a forensic pathologist.

In the film *Fingered*, directed by Richard Kern, star and collaborator Lunch digs deep into her psycho-sexual fascination with unending raw power. When co-star Marty Nation sticks his fingers—lubricated with rotten black sump oil—deep into her asshole a line is crossed, the viewer is compelled to address his or her own understanding of sexual pleasure, the notion of consent and limits. The film makes it clear during its opening scene, that it is "catering only to our own preferences as members of the sexual minority".

The artist views her desire as an essential manifestation of what she frequently refers to as her "sickness", sexual need evinced as a festering red rash needing to be constantly scratched. Here concupiscence emerges free of repression, the physic autocracy of the humanist subject submerged beneath the purity of the need to feel at whatever price.

In her visual art Lydia Lunch adopts an instinctive approach, the temporal *viva voce* that defines her music, spoken word, and film could not exist in the framed stasis of the photographic image, which necessitated a different form of engagement. Unconcerned with technical niceties, her images are multifarious, existing not in one simple style but as a series of ongoing experiments whether naturalistic, abstracted, or experimental, whether celluloid or digital. What they have in common is the same intensity as her written and musical work, manifested in a rigorously focused gaze. Each picture attempts to peel back the veneer, to examine the psychology that lies beneath, opening up that which has been repressed for meticulous examination.

Her earliest photographs are almost traditional portraits depicting the teens who hung around her New Orleans neighbourhood. Caught in the fragile imminence of the endless grey summer between childhood and adulthood, these images attempt to capture the possibility of the future yet realised. Simultaneously Lunch began photographing abandoned houses, shotgun shacks, and the detritus found in empty urban lots. These decaying wooden buildings, rusty cars, and rotten piss soiled mattresses became a series of photographs originally described as *Scenes Of Crimes Yet To Be Committed*. Places pregnant with nihilistic potential and raw beauty.

If these works are concerned with a history that is not yet written then Lunch's photographs of the ruins of the Spanish town of Belchite take the opposite approach, digging through the weight of ruins searching the traces of history, trauma, geography, and landscape. Belchite—where in two bloody weeks in August 1937 an estimated 6,000 people were killed—the ruined landscape and charnel fields a precursor to the unleashed all-to-human slaughter of the Second World War. Lunch's photographs of the town render the landscape, the skeletal ruins, and the rot of collapsing buildings as pure traumascape, as a slaughterhouse carved deep into the psyche.

History may be about archaeology, about digging in the dirt, but in the traumascape if there is digging to be done it will be on all fours, scrabbling with bloodied knuckles into the hard, dry, sun-baked soil. If warfare has defined society then it has also revealed an unpleasant truth about humanity. War is the hell from which our societies have emerged and to which they will eventually return. However in this promise of destruction there exists the possibility of beauty, amongst this rubble there is a fragile aesthetic.

"THEY OUTLAWED EVERYTHING THAT SPELLED PLEASURE."

Meltdown (Lydia Lunch, *Stinkfist*)

The seductive nature of crime and the stink of cruel potential informs the collaboration with photographer, criminologist, and sometimes professional pool shark, Marc Viaplana. Exhibited as *The Scene Of The Crime Could Be Anywhere At Anytime* the work documents the years of Lunch and Viaplana's relationship. If photographs exist as a visual record, then these images are *memento muerte*; stolen criminal moments where lust and violence collide and charting Lunch and Viaplana's relationship as it twists like a black gyre from the stinking back alleys of Los Angeles to cheap apartments in Barcelona, Bonnie and Clyde style. The two artists share a desire to exist at an extreme, howling into the abyss of mortality as they transverse the globe, leaving nothing behind but traces of cum and blood—a confession of DNA. The act of fucking emerges as a criminal gesture, a moment when everything becomes possible even as it is erased.

The photograph has formed a crucial part of crime scene forensics since the early twentieth century, but with Lunch and Viaplana the image is not just a form of evidence but a celebration of the act of transgression. For the artists the desire for evidence both motivates and enables the breaking of laws.

This personal exploration informs Lunch's most clearly experimental photographs. Unlike previous series of images which were shot for exhibition, these pictures were constructed initially to be used as projected backdrops for 'illustrated word' performances. In contrast to the *Scene Of The Crime* series, and by necessity of purpose, these images are contained within the rectangular frame. The content reflects an engagement with the Surrealist demand that art represents fantasies, desires, dreams and the fluidity between these internal desires and conscious thought, the titles of the images from the *Hieromancy* series repeatedly draw attention to these themes: *Third Eye* and *Fever Dreams*. Conversely the psychic dislocation associated with lack of sleep inform the title *Insomniac Theatre*, once again drawing attention to the breakdown of the distinction between reality and fantasy.

Visually this experimental work retains a luminescence, but the digitally manipulated colour, rich in primary tones, the use of shadow, and the blur of the multiple images necessitates the viewer look carefully. It becomes necessary to engage with each scotopic nuance in order to fully experience the fluidity and liminality of the multiple images. The photographs are about vague forms and ghostly images—weapons blur with images of oral sex in *Killer Urge*, a stairwell combines with a vagina in the aptly titled *Luminal*—the 'base' nature of the themes reflected in the tones of the image, creating a dark luminosity. The relationship between unconscious urges and conscious experience are mutable, fantasy both the reason and engine for behaviour.

Uniquely amongst these images *My Death Waits There* appears as a collection of photographs reflecting and echoing each other in a quasi-symmetrical form. The light entering is bright but there is nothing to be seen outside, beyond overexposed echoes of the same industrial nothingness. The barren rooms and empty warehouse space a series of dark places that reek of filthy blocked drains, burnt dust motes, and the desperate hot wet fucks of teenagers and winos. An actuality of both interior and exterior territories, this collection of images, appears almost as a votive, an actualisation of fear and desire for the promise of destruction.

Finally, it is not possible to delineate a clear distinction between annihilation and eroticism in Lunch's work, the two function as part of the same necessary gesture towards the simultaneous affirmation and eradication of the self. Freedom demands risk and the freedom of the unleashed passions entails the possibility of destruction.

In this respect Lunch's art recalls Federico Garcia Lorca's evocation of the Duende, a force for artistic creation that does not simply come from outside; like the seduction promised by the muse or spiritual enlightenment offered by an angel, but from "the nethermost recesses of the blood". Lorca, a sexual transgressor and outsider who would be murdered in cold blood by homophobic fascists, wrote of the Duende as a creativity that draws blood, exhausts and repulses "all the bland, geometrical assurances". The Duende emerges only at the understanding, the immanence of death, evoked through the artist subsuming themselves completely within the process of creation.

Jack Sargeant

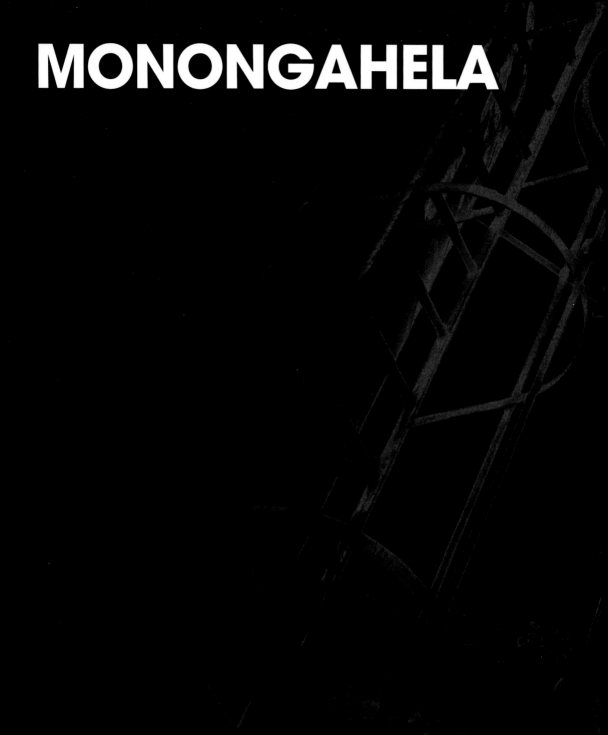

MONONGAHELA

MONONGAHELA

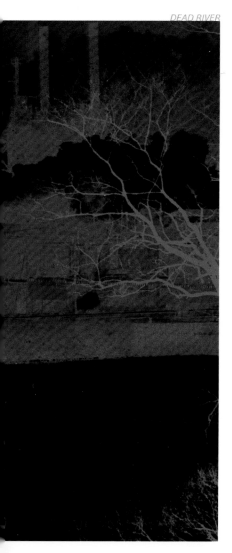

DEAD RIVER

Night stalking dead zones. Rummaging through
the ghostly remnants of ravaged villages.
The wreckage of life dispossessed. Decayed
orphans whose guts have been ripped out
and sold for scraps. Slivers of copper wiring
scattered like auburn gossamer refracting
sunlight. Empty hollows which suck life into its
vortex. Existing as testament to mystery and
disappearance. Forming a beautiful vacuum
devoid of humans. This is bliss.

SOUTHSIDE

MONONGAHELA

MCKEES ROCK

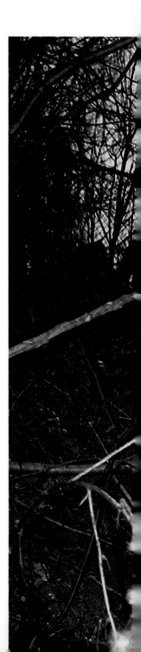

THE PRICE YOU PAY

MONONGAHELA

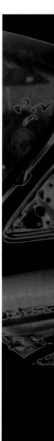

ALL MY HEROES
ARE KILLERS

ADAM

I have spent months, possibly years, comatose
on park benches tracking the periphery of
playgrounds, skulking through shopping malls,
falling asleep in the library, attempting to
trap a fleeting image. The image of a young
boy captured at just the right moment. That
transient fleeting second when a certain
amount of natural light falls on the hollows
of his cheeks. Casts an effervescent glow.
A splash of sunlight dancing on his lips. To
rebirth within me that blossom of purity etched
deep within their innocent smile.

There's something about how fine their
bones are. Under their flesh. The possibility
of shattering them under my need. Skin
pulled tight around bony joints. The flattering
reflection of my own beauty divorced of disease
and sickness. A temporary vacation from the
devastation that has ringed the wellspring of
my life.

Not that I could ever forget how much of my own life has already been melted away. How much I gave up, gave over, wasted. How much has already been stolen. Destroyed. How many rope burns have left their browning residue around my heart strings. You don't have to fight yourself too hard to fall in love. At least for an hour. 20 minutes. Two days. A week. With a young boy who finds in you the love they never found in their own mothers arms. And reciprocates it twofold. I'll play Mommie. I need to and I'm good at it. There's nothing to lose and what it is you gain is their life force. A transformation. Salvation. A resurrection. A day off from playing wet nurse in the trauma unit nursing damage junkies back to health.

ADAM AND ALEJANDRO

RUSTY

LEO

DYLAN

DYLAN

EDDY

JOHNNY

ADAM

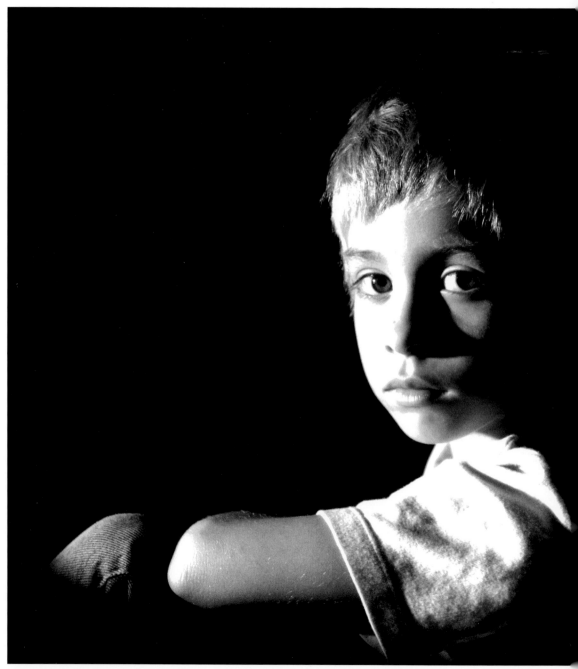

JIMMY

FATAL BEAUTY

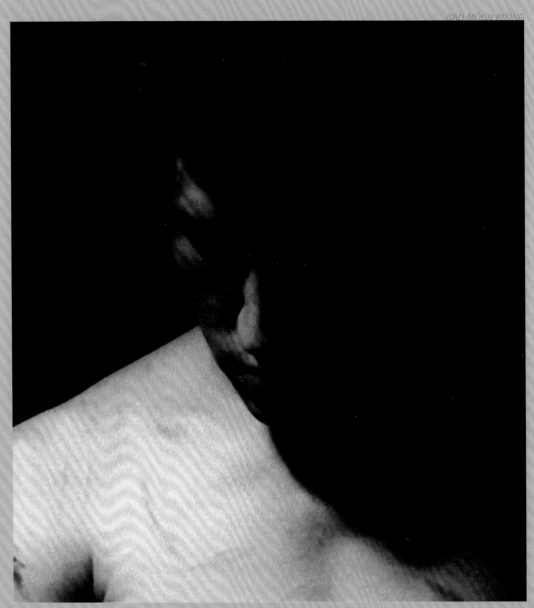

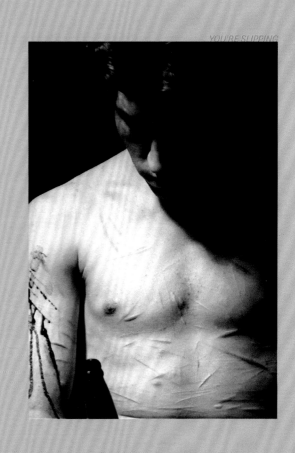

If the inside of your head gets pummeled with enough emotional blunt force trauma to splinter the psyche you develop ways to punish the body—that fleshy prison which houses the pain.

Your trusty friend the razor will never
tell a single lie.

The body as experimental canvas
as blood bank
as punching bag
as carving board
as sack of pus and cum.

I am an endangered species
suicided by society
justifiably paranoid
rife with contradictions.

An open wound bled sensitive
by the corrosive indifference
of a world battered into numbness.
Ignorant in its inability to recognise
the magnetic force fields of a technology
which poisons the soul
creating a moral pollution,
a psychic vacuum, a spiritual void
overflowing with infectious toxic runoff.

The body as carrier. A cantankerous cavern
filled with fear and loathing. A prison riddled
with the cancer of being. Held captive by invisible forces
who cohabitate in conspiracy to abolish the individual.

THE DEATH
OF INNOCENCE

YOU MADE ME

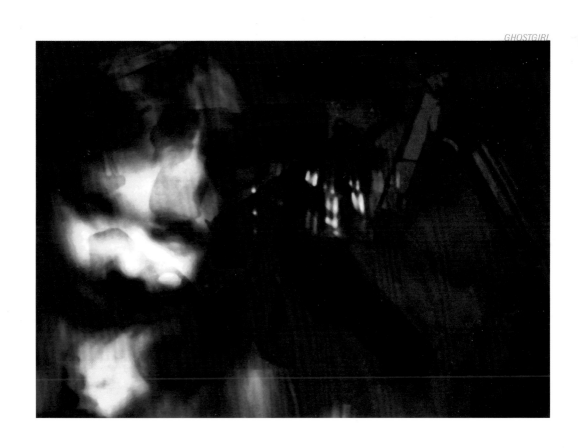

THE DEATH OF INNOCENCE

SLEEPWALKER

RETRIBUTION

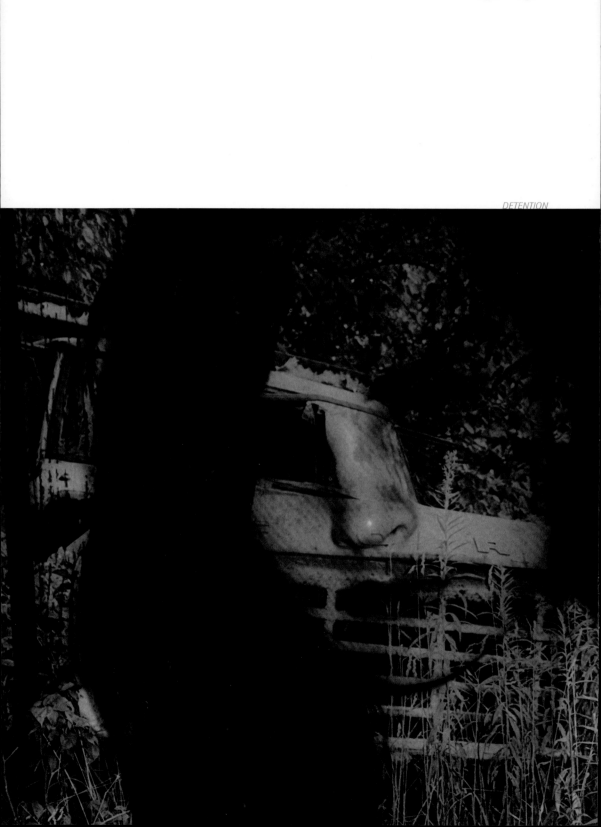

BREAKOUT

HIEROMANCY

AN ITCH IN INNER SPACE...
A VORTEX BETWEEN MUSCLE AND BONE
WHICH EXPANDS INCHES FEET MILES BEYOND THE SKIN
LONG LOST SACRED GEOMETRY
REFLECTING INVISIBLE CIRCLES OF LIGHT
ASYMMETRICAL PATTERNS WHOSE SECERT CODES
REBEL AGAINST DEFINITION

ELEMENTAL

I'm stranded in a dream state being tracked by beautiful
corpses. They're seducing me with soft smiles which hide
rotten teeth and sour breath. Whispering sexy innuendoes and
offering up a powdered narcotic. Their attempts to viperise
me in order to decode my magick makes my spine prickle as
these subhuman aphrodisiacs put the make on me making
goo goo eyes and cooing like lovesick homing pigeons. The
dream drugs must be working. Floating through a maze of
flesh coloured passageways peopled with slutty robots whose
inflamed erogenous zones and exaggerated perversions lend an
almost sultry residue to whatever surface their attentions melt
up against. They want a piece of whatever it is that lurks directly
below the surface of my skin as if they're trying to crawl under
and get inside that razor thin layer of epidermis where my smell
emanates from.

THIS FLESHY VEHICLE UNDULATES
PANIC AND ECSTASY FUEL THE FLAMES
THE GHOST OF YOUR SEX LEAVES THE PILLOW STAINED
AND NOW THERE'S BLOOD ON THE SHEETS AGAIN

NUMB NARCOSIS SLEEP STEALS DREAMS
THE BODY AS A NEED MACHINE
CRAWLS IN BED WITH THE ENEMY
MORPHEUS AND MEPHISTOPHELES

WHITE LIGHT MIGRAINE BRAINFREEZE BURN
ASHES AND ETHER A CHEMICAL BLUR
LONG NIGHTS THAT YOU LIVE TO FORGET
THE GHOST OF YOUR SEX PLAYING RUSSIAN ROULETTE

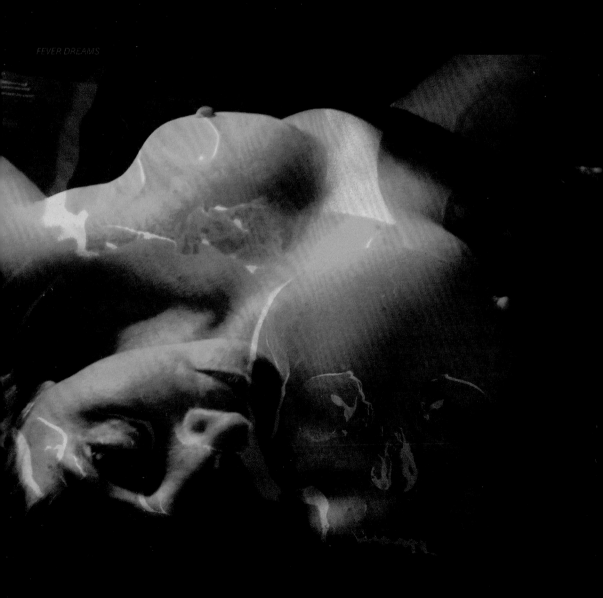

FEVER DREAMS

REROMANCY

Fever Dreams.
To murder yourself with memories
To swelter in this midnight of madness
A sick ghost imprisoned in flesh
Whose mouth screams your name

Libido violates petty convention
Splattering with blood
The bones of inhibitions

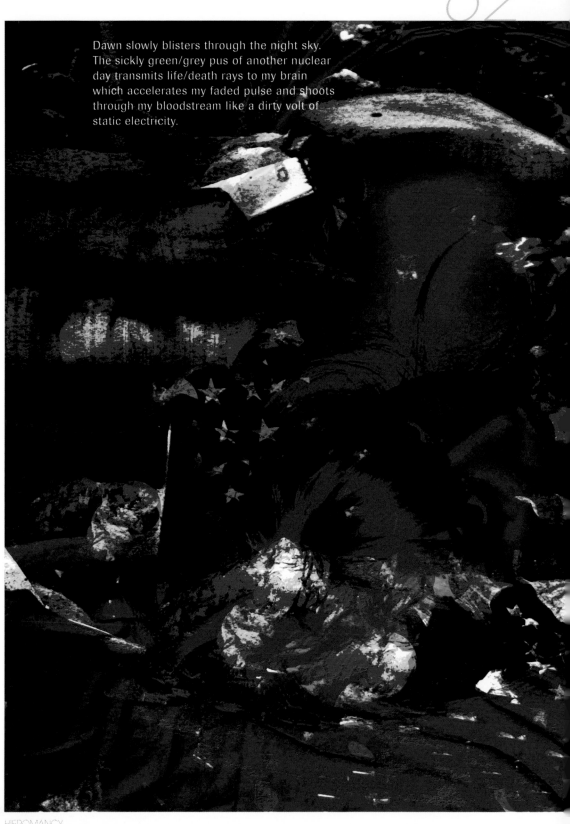

Dawn slowly blisters through the night sky.
The sickly green/grey pus of another nuclear
day transmits life/death rays to my brain
which accelerates my faded pulse and shoots
through my bloodstream like a dirty volt of
static electricity.

SPECTROPHILIA

"You stretch out your hand in the dark and you don't know who or what will take it."
Hilary Mantel

Of course I long to be
The laziest bitch in the whorehouse...
Legs spread wide, head turned to one side
Lucky Strike dangling from my
Cock stained scarlet lips
Eyes on the alarm clock
Whose somnambulant throb
Reminds me with every pulsation
That my heartbeat has slowed to a death march
Whose funereal procession will be
A century long samba
Littered with the beautiful corpses
Of hundreds of dead soldiers
Who had come to soil my battlefield
With their heavy artillery
Pumping into me like bullets
Fired at point blank range
Anointed with the hot molten lead
Which would mingle with the blood and cum
Eyes heavy with morphine, cocaine, MDMA or madness
Mind swill drunk on the uncountable contaminants
Whose steady diet I have feasted on for decades
As a tribute to my own survival of the sickest.

Blood is just memory without language
The sins of the flesh are just a sacrifice to Venus
Passion plays itself out in the killing zone of false memory
All these secrets they just stain my recollections

THE PROMISE OF PARADISE

The Big Picture projected on a small screen
made of flesh and bone gone bad
long before the graveyard.
A thoughtographic hologram
heavy as a freight train
bathed in the blood of Martyrs.
Every few seconds
a new temptation
asserts itself.
Another evil snicker
awful chortle
tap on the glass
knock on the door
stamp on the floor.
Begging to be let in
let out
unleashed
released
freed from the prison
of their silent hell.
A solitary confinement
shut up in an isolation tank
like sick sharks shedding teeth
and tails
shrouded in a bouquet
of blood and sinew
muscle and pus.
Singing the song of the sirens
to the janitors of lunacy
who are down dredging the swamps
in search of a new life
new light
a different kind
of midnight.

93

Consider the thought of re-incarnation
as the ability to dissect the secret history
inherent in our genetic coding and the
multiple atrocities which have polluted our
bloodlines. Contemplate suffering as an acute
oversensitivity to geography. Imagine that every
stone, stairwell and street has absorbed the
life, death and fear of everyone that has come
before you and your job is to give voice to this
nightmare. This is my murder.

Open to the elements
I bend with time and night steals in
Locked inside a velvet cove
A dreamless state that I call home

I'm sleeping with his ghost. If I roll my eyes far
enough back in my head letting just the sliver
of white like a cracked crescent moon kiss the
morning somewhere under my bloodshot lids
I'll zero in on him and like a cheap five and
dime store front gypsy fortune teller I'll read
his last thought and it will scare the living shit
out of me.

ALCHEMICAL

BABY'S ON FIRE

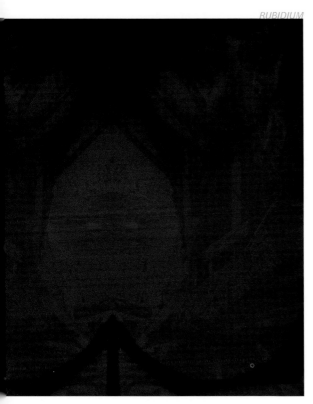

The art of ritual and masquerade
Line the skin like artificial nerves
Sin is just a trick on niggers
And we're all niggers
Broken on the wheel of fate
Shackled to what never was
What never will be
Haunted again and again
By the ghosts of a murdered conscience

Where sex is now an act of murder

Delirious spasms
Toxic hallucinations
The delicious languor of disintegration
I can smell it coming
Like fallout from some terrible explosion
Scattered by the wind
A siren sings out
Recognise the song from the tombs
It's calling you

I'm in a place where reason went missing
Where do you turn to
When everything inside you
Resists paradise
And you feel stuck inside an oasis
Of horror and boredom
Looking for a small pocket
To disappear into
But tiny wisps of someone else's thoughts
Project magnetic impulses
And ego that lucid viper
Bites like a snake
Whose secrets make you sick

INSOMNIAC
THEATRE

I am the ghost in the woodwork
An interstitial conduit within the hollow
Inverse to the absence of visible life
My night vision takes flight
Reverses back in and releases me
Into the broken arms of empty space
Where I am embraced like a memory
Who haunts the shattered face
Of a battered room

TRY ME

My private museum. Filled floor to ceiling with
masterpieces I create in invisible ink sketched
by fingernail into the canvas of my flesh.
A nonstop rotating film loop replicating Reubens
Bruegels Bosch Bellini Bernini Goya Caravaggio.

The Masters—whose subjects not unlike myself
were forced by circumstances beyond their
control into playing victim at the hands of cruel
gods and vicious monsters whose only offering
of salvation beyond this tortured existence
was in the knowledge that a suffering that
wounds beyond the shallow exterior of flesh
and bone penetrating through the multiple
levels of epidermis into and beyond every fiber
of your being an agony from which no solitary
moment without would ever again be complete
is offered up in loving submission to a greater
being. A being with no equal. Whose God-like
powers and omnipotent understanding no
matter how cruelly projected or simultaneously
you are rejected from it is reward unto itself.

On my 33rd birthday
I had a .357 in my mouth.

The bitter taste of gunmetal still coats my tongue
Tickles my throat and screams your name.

I have now made a tentative agreement
with some of the more obstreperous personalities
which stalk the fleshy mansion which I inhabit.

If they agree not to run naked though the streets
bleeding and beseeching
If they refuse the urge to hang themselves
from the chandelier of an abandoned hotel
on the outskirts of the desert
If they promise not to disembowel themselves
in the morgue of an abandoned nineteenth century
forensics facility that has crumbled under the rubble
If they inhale only a miniscule amount
of poisonous gas or nitroaromatic compounds
If they do not conspire to stage a revolt
and nail themselves to a tree 275 yards
from the nearest roadway as tasty morsel
to a pack of wild coyotes...
then and only then...
will I let them out to play with you.

STREET SWEEPER

I play dumb. Sit across from them on the train, the bus, the street corner, a stoop and drain my eyes of the truth. Turn the murky violet a crystal clear azure. Flood the iris with an irresistible innocence. Perfect fraud. Pout. Thrusting out my lower lip. Just a bit. Bite it. Softly. Show the tip of my tongue. Just the tip. Put on a baby face. Erase 20 years of violence, cruelty and apathy. Fake interest. Curiosity. Wonder. Awe. Tilt my head a little to the left. Play with my hair. Fidget on the bench, in my seat, on the stairs. Wiggle my ass like a little kitten. Open my eyes even wider. Smile. Showing pointy little teeth that could rip their fucking throats out. They drown in a stupid fantasy I have forced into their head like a viral infection which spirals them into my vortex. They swallow the bait like bottom feeders glutting on an orgy of fresh krill.

KILLER URGE

LUMINAL

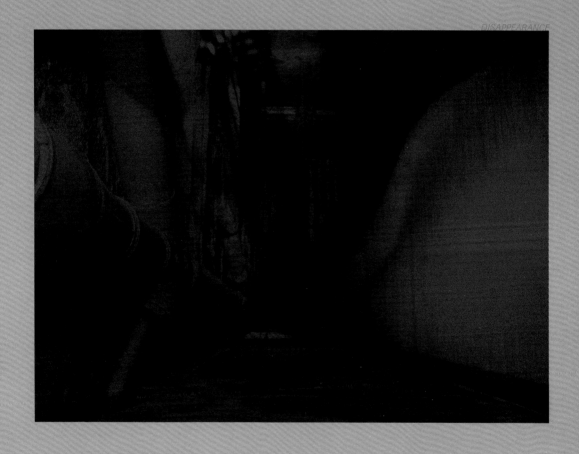

THE SICKNESS
OF STRANGERS

Late night lost in that haunted no man's land
Stranded at the corner of Sunset and Occidental
The ghosts of all those who could've been...
Leave a vaseline smeared lipstick smudge
On the rear view mirror's blood stained crack

Lonely as one left shoe with a broken ankle strap
Pitched out the window of the Starlight Motel
No drug potent enough to kill off the vision of you
That soured honey tumbleweed of hair
Which smells of dirty sex and cigarettes

Your kiss is burned into my lips
Like a faded hologram slightly out of focus
I keep reaching for your mouth forgetting
How the night bled out turning an angel
Into a beautiful corpse who curses my memory

Johnny bruises a tender ache inside of me.
Even after an all night bender when he comes
swaggering back to my bunk, bent on an ugly
kind of drunk, stinking of Wild Irish Rose,
sporting another black eye and limping again,
the way his face lights up when he knows I'm
half awake, been waiting up staring down the
clock, sucking up caffeine and codeine, worried
sick and swollen from not enough sleep and
pissed off yeah, pissed, but still thrilled, can't
fake a cock on because I just want a kiss, and
he gets to live another day, so I get to live
another day, which is all the reason I need to
forgive him at least for now.

Johnny crawls into bed bloody and beer stained. He's cut himself again. I pretend I'm still sleeping. He feels closer to me, safer, he can relax when I'm half dead. He cradles into my coma. Cupping my whole body from behind. It calms him down, slows his blood. He presses himself against me. His thick leather belt sweats against my back. He buries his face in my hair. Inhales slowly. Supping on my dusky aroma. A dirty white honeysuckle stained with night's runoff.

I am the oxygen that he feeds on. A cleansing hallucinogen. The undercurrent of musky heat radiates life into his open mouth. When he's with me he can breathe again. I feel his excitement building. Long slow deep breaths grow shallow, hollow. The air catches fire in his dry cottony throat. He swallows, mouths "I want so badly to love you like you pretend to love me" I tremble. Frozen.

I want to lash out, thrash against him, scream his name. Pound his temples. Smash him in the face. Shoot him in the fucking head. Stab his lower lip, his arms, his legs, his back and chest. Cut him into a thousand crimson ribbons so that he would, for that one moment, truly comprehend just how much I do love him. How badly I want him, how needy I really am. How Hungry. How incredibly moist.

Johnny could stubbornly avoid sleep for 46, 68, 72 hours at a time. Propelled by alcohol, speed, coke, adrenaline or just sheer panic, he'd string himself so far out he could barely light a cigarette. Raise a bottle. Trembling hands massaging a leg spasm. Chapped lips cracked by pointy canines. X-ray eyes detecting invisible monsters who'd steal him from me as he night stalked energy trails, falling stars, fading headlights, meteors, night birds, stray cats. Flashlight cocked to hip, butcher knife in torn back pocket. Sneak peeping around corners. Frozen in door frames. Glued to the window sill, peeking through a cigarette burn in the fabric. Paralysed at the foot of the stairs. Paranoid agitation strangled the hours. Fuelled his psychosis. Bored the shit out of me.

He would attempt to decode the flow of traffic two blocks away, the scampering of rats in the next building, an ant hill under construction in the back yard. An insane reconnaissance mission. The enemy... a sonic surround. Every creaky floorboard, rattling pipe, electrical hum, a forged television static which seemed to leak from his ears out. Filling the room with a reverberating symphony of sub-decibel tones only he could hear. A swelling claustrophobia. The cold sweat on his brow expanding like a freak weather pattern which coated the room in a dense fog of atmospheric perspiration.

This is forced up from the world of whispers
Where terror and negation
Are out on an endless prowl
I'm just attempting to summon
The memory of pre-epidemic existence
While nursing bruised ideals
Which combat human short comings

We are all transitional creatures
Who destroy ourselves in slow motion
In our terror and in our ignorance
We do the very things
Which aggravate the calamity
And increase the death rate

The interval separating you from your corpse
is a small sticky wound

Each fate
Is no more than a refrain
Fluttering around a few bloodstains
And nothing can keep you from bleeding
Ideas themselves turn red
And encroach upon us like tumors
In some kind of philosophical stupor

YOU ARE NOT SAFE IN YOUR OWN HOME

Imagine a fight club for fucking. An atmosphere that stinks of wet sex. A room that is littered with the detritus of need, soiled by the stigma of black lust. This is the raw wound of a need that is greater than romantic love, but lacking the self-identified discourse of the victim.

Lunch's bed is covered in stained sheets. Blood. Dirt. And yellowing dry shots of cum. Sleep never happened here. This is not a bedroom that allows for quasi-shocked titillation, no condom packets here. This is fucking where safety is not on the agenda, bodily fluids are exchanged and blood is shed.

Next to the bed a black-and-white television plays a loop of homemade porn, But never to the visual climax of male ejaculation, the evidence that completes and closes most video-pornography. Instead the action loops into an endless parade of female masturbatory copulation. The video has been cropped in order to both deny identity to the male combatant, and in essence to demote him to the ranks of everyman. A brutal lesson elevated to Theater of Cruelty, whereby the artist as predator is immersing herself in momentary oblivion, entering animal brain, eradicating individuality to taste the infinite.

Desire here is articulated not just through the moans of female sexual pleasure accompanying the video, but also through the black and white image of the male-object pinned to the wall. His violence is directed everywhere, especially at his own fleshy cage, his muscular body is brutally dissected, skin cut away to exorcise and exercise his pain. This is a torso that bares 200 self inflicted scars. Like the wounds gouged into his chest this installation exists to remind the audience of mortality and desire. Lustmord is reworked as the twisted convulsions of the slow suicide because every act is racing towards that ultimate end. The ultimate fuck. A violent collision of damaged body parts and tortured emotions battling against each other in the condensed space of a finite time.

"The battle of sex as an animal act fucked up by your emotions" spray painted in black towering overhead. Revenge against a violent juvenalia of misspent emotions.

Jack Sargeant

YOU ARE NOT SAFE IN YOUR OWN HOME

"There's a thin line between a love tap and murder with a blunt instrument".

I've always had an overwhelming compulsion to confess, to reveal the most revolting details of my existence to others. I possess a criminal predilection, devoid of guilt which insists I admit to not only my own crimes of passion, but also my complicity in aggravating others to commit crimes both for and against me.

I play judge, jury, convict and victim. A schizophrenic passion play that feeds on the intoxicating repercussions of the repetitive cycle of abuse. An unending theme in my body of work.

From my earliest lyrics, spoken word performances and films, I have sung vicious incantations bemoaning the cruel fate of the human condition, where each of us bears some mark of battery.

We have all been victimised at some point because of our gender, race, age, social or economic status, religion or lack thereof. Our first cry is slapped out of us as we are violently wrenched from the relative safety of the crimson universe deep within our mother's bodies. Born in blood and battered into breathing, life begins with brutality and baptizes with violence.

Violence is an addictive electrical current which burns at both ends. Cruel lessons taught within the torture chamber of the nuclear family, which are replayed with systematic repetition over and over again in our adult relationships until we are able to recognise the patterning of ritualised abuse and readdress our participation in its ongoing cycle.

My goal has always been to, if not step off the wheel, away from the scaffold, out from under the guillotine of genetically pre-programmed trauma bonds, to at least recognise that I am not the only one living under a life sentence of victimhood. Willing or not. I seek to illustrate this eternal dilemma and give voice to those who like myself, are forever sick with desire.

SHADOWHOURS

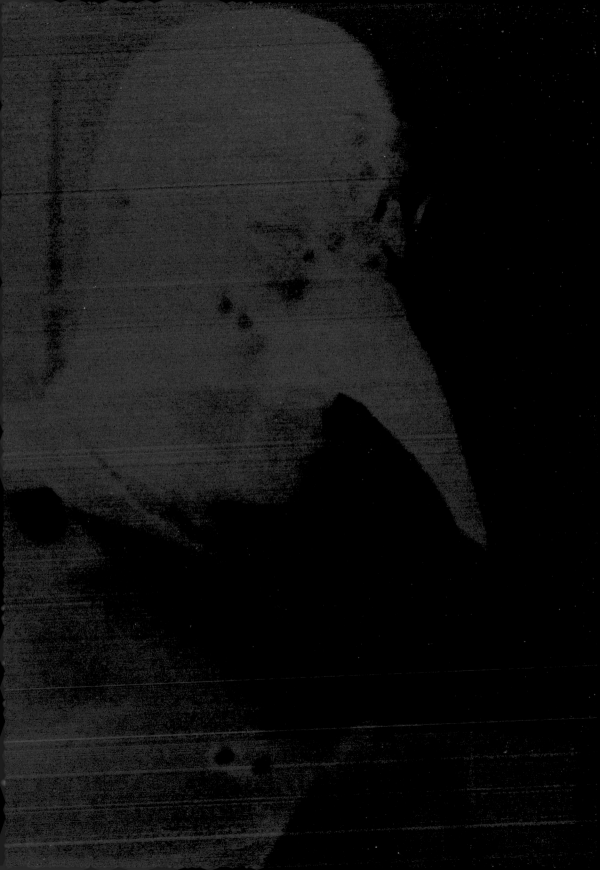

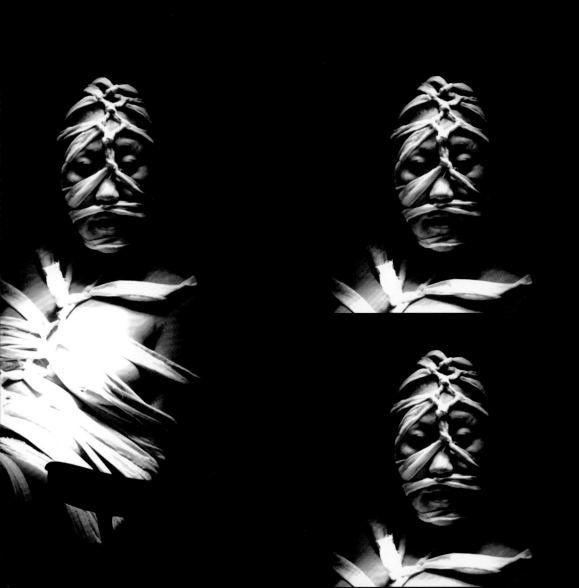

This hollow tomb where love comes to bloom—
A receptacle of panic and ecstasy
Lust and disease
A ravaged temple
A way station for so many monsters
Contaminated by a polluted bloodline
A road map of ancient bruises
A whipping post
Condemned as heir to the flagellants
Cursed by all of History's agonies
Nailed to myself
Stricken with the rapture of disgust

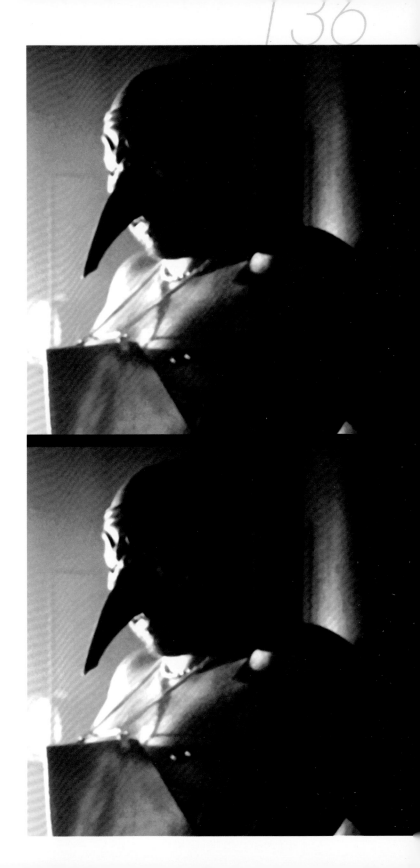

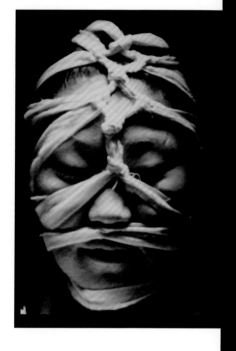

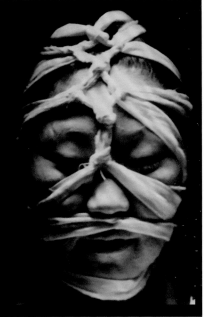

The void is just an inverted dream in which we are all engulfed. Doomed to the empty hours of eternity to the periphery of shudders and mildewed desires where idiot savants wander the wasteland in search of lost love among the ruined. What you call love I call a duel of saliva between perfumed corpses who seek to accelerate their own destruction and display their wounds under the beams of a luminous chancre. I long for the insincerities of the flesh that furnace of blood and guts with the gift of tears. I love watching lovers profit from their sickness exploiting their disequilibrium with violence and skill in the salon of blood and guts that boneyard of dreams where the extremities of passion and rapture rupture into an abscess an absence the dismal abyss which follows delirium.

CRYSTALISED

THE SCENE OF THE CRIME COULD BE ANYWHERE AT ANY TIME

Somebody broke in
But all that was missing were the Poloraids

The scene of the crime could be anywhere at any time...

And I'm always salivating about the maniac responsible
I know that to attack is merely the desire
To free one's self from infatuation
That there's a thin line between a love tap
And murder with a blunt instrument
That a sharp stick in the eye
Kills the devil in the soul every time

I'm always lacerating myself with memories
And the demented visions of some woe-begotten
Messenger of the Lord whose now living down at the
Hangover Hotel where everybody's living hand to mouth
Trying to get ahead—but shit—a quick jaunt down to the corner store
To pick up a 40 of Colt 45, a fifth of Jack, a bottle of aspirins
Half a dozen condoms and a carton of cigarettes—
Will bring you down real hard by about 150 bucks
And then all you're left with is your dreams...
And you'll be dreaming amongst drunks

Yeah dreaming...

Remembering the way it used to be... the way it used to be...
Shit... the way it still is... dirt cheap deeds sloppily executed
On sheetless mattresses... petty crimes of passion
Bringing secrets to the surface with blood and alcohol...

The scene of the crime could be anywhere at any time

THE SCENE OF THE CRIME COULD BE ANYWHERE AT ANY TIME

TOMORROW IS JUST A WORD FOR A PLACE WE'RE ALL LOOKING FOR

MAC 10

FULL AUTO

I admit it.
The American Way of Life has turned me into
A death defying murder junkie
Whose own death is the ultimate sexual turn on
And the closer I get to death
The more energy I have to fight against it
You're either with me or against me

Do you want to fight or do you want to fuck

I get drunk on disasters, calamities, casualties
I'm high on bombs bursting in air
Rifles ricocheting off the bellies of pregnant women
The bombing of abortion clinics
Crippled children poisoned on a school bus
Shopping mall murders, crumbling cities polluted beyond repair
Craters of despair in the eyes of men, women and children
Their brains rotted by the cathode glare of the television
The Internet and video games which only mimic a world gone wild
Where high school campuses have become the practice range
For soldiers of misfortune who have been programmed
To search and destroy

Where all the killers are heroes
All the heroes are killers

RECOIL

UPLOAD

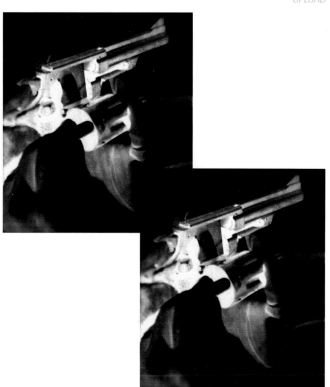

Man has turned the world into a ghetto, a whorehouse
An orphanage, a refugee camp, a sweatshop, a slaughterhouse
A bomb factory, a landmine, a butcher shop, a shooting gallery
An insane asylum, a gas chamber, a toxic fucking dump

And I myself am filled with a MURDEROUS RAGE
Gang Warfare waged under my skin
A battle of bitches boxing their way out

I have become the rapist whose impotence
At annihilating the real killers is manifested
Into violence against myself
And anyone else who gets in my fucking way

A passion killer riddled with criminal urges
A sadist incarcerated in her own torture chamber
One minute you're flesh and blood
And the next you're flesh and bones
Piles and piles of flesh and bones
And if you think I'm hostile—
You have no fucking clue just how much
Self control I execute

My war has always been
The battle of sex as an animal act
Fought hand to gland
One woman against every man

I've gotten inside the enemy's head
I'm sleeping in his fucking bed
My womb a tomb a sacrificial cunt
The more they kill
The more I fuck

EVIDENCE

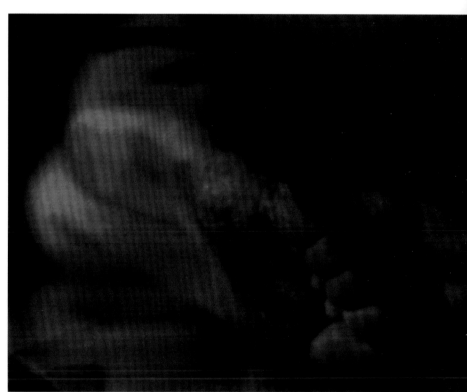

And when, not if, but when
They drop the fucking bomb on my head
Because I could become their next target—
I plan on dying with a smile on my face
Laughing in delight, smoking a fat joint
Blowing a dozen lines of cocaine
Tripping on MDMA
And fucking half a dozen returning Iraqi war vets—
Somebody has got to take care of the amputees

I pity the idiot ridiculous enough to pray for heaven
The fool who dreams of life everlasting
I want my fix of paradise and I want it now
And the more you have the more you want
And more is never enough

Which is why the Devil granted me this celestial body
And the face of an Angel
So that I could do her bidding in blessing
All the little bitch boys with a christ complex to
Eat of my flesh
Drink of my blood
Come unto my ALTAR

MY DEATH WAITS THERE

THE SCENE OF THE CRIME COULD BE ANYWHERE AT ANY TIME

Welcome to my Church
The Church of the Unholy Redeemer
Where the only Commandment is Pleasure

Pleasure at the mouth of the Apocalypse
Ecstasy at the brink of the Disaster

I always wanted Ecstasy and I finally found it
I must find Ecstasy in this insanity
Freedom from their slavery
The Truth in their lies
Beauty in their destruction
Peace in the homicidal genocide of the
War whore's evil orgy of death and negation
Love amongst the ruins
Pleasure in my own pain

ARCHITECT
OF DESIRE

It takes a master alchemist...
It takes a master alchemist to create a functional stability
between the contamination of genetic mutation, environmental hazards,
moral pollution, hormonal imbalance and toxic emotions from which I struggle

My daily existence is a battlecade of extreme fluctuations
where chaos clobbers apathy which beats the shit out of depression
which follows irritability which slams into anger which eclipses ecstasy
which slips through my fingers far too often

Ecstasy slips through my fingers far too often

I'm still searching for the drug which can trigger euphoria

I had my first mood swing while still in the womb when the the bliss of non-being
was shattered by the bullrun of my father's bloodline—that bastard's insanity—
brutally crashing through my fragile endocranial

The inside of my head has been punching the shit out of itself since I was a child.
Migraines rebel against my internal landscape, that sewer of muscle, meat, sinew
and blood, which stinks of sulfur and rose water

I'm still searching for the drug

My brainpan overflows with ancient memories
which have fractured into splintered obsidian
only to be melted into tiny hammers
whose thunder roars out of my mouth

SWEAT FACTORY 1

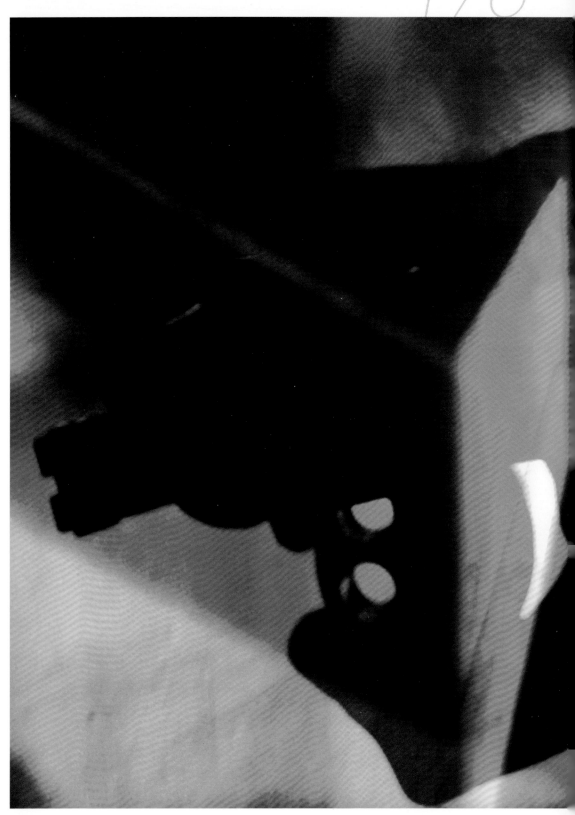

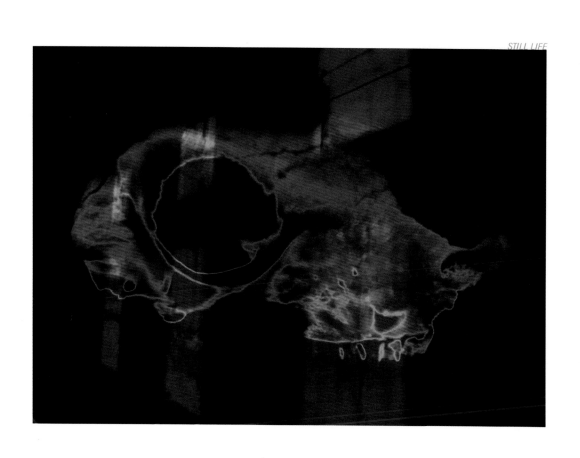

How long would it take to walk yourself to death? Would you shoot a hole in your hand to drink your own blood if you were stranded on an endless sand plain, the only sign of life—what's left of your own?

Escape is essential. I flee to avoid capture, to temporarily outrun retribution.
I strive to calculate the distance of miles between the past and the future,
a futile attempt to manipulate the time I will spend forever stuck in a permanent limbo.

The desert speaks to the fugitive in me.
A godless gunman. Isolated. Alone.
A mysterious apparition with a burning desire to obliterate everyone and everything. A one man holocaust of infinite destruction who renders the landscape not blood red, but burnt umber, a patina that speaks of the absence of colour, the absence of life. The empty husk of an eternal hollow.

An Insomniac's Theatre of dream states and nightmares haunted by an army of vagrant ghosts and invisible enemies who make ruin everything in their wake.

Freedom is a solitary state of grace, an oasis glistening somewhere off in the twilight horizon. Where the shackles that bind have been blown to bits by the bull end of a Tommy Gun. But is anyone ever truly free if he can't shake off his shadow? Can't kill off his own bitter fantasies or brutal delusions?

The Deadman inhabits a parallel universe where a primordial essence stalks patiently. Eternally hunting. An intercessor standing motionless exiled to a dusty terrain. A twilight hell of his own making.

A barren panorama from which all life has been leeched. It weeps of desolation, the desert and death. A man, a murderer, alone. Imprisoned in thought. Hounded as if by locusts, a numbing din, a deep subterranean rumble. A lifetime of despicable secrets forever murmuring just out of earshot.

I am that man. That rouse, the ruin. Ruptured.

A magnificent wreck. A mirage located far South of No North. In this enticing envelope of devil winds if I looked to you as I truly am you would never be able to see me for I would no longer exist. I would have been erased, evaporated, turned back into dust and blown away upon the desert shore.

This battlefield where I am pitted against myself. Against my memories and their recriminations. My brutality and its empty other. From this siege there is no fitful sleep. No relief. Only unholy rest in which I tremble. Hostaged by futility, treachery, aggression. Exhausted and numb. Waking again and again to be blistered by sun, consumed in sand, and left alone to battle my shadow.

MACUMBA

YOUR GHOST STINKS UP EVERYTHING

LANDSCAPES
AFTER THE BATTLE

*"My exile was not only a physical one, motivated exclusively by political reasons;
it was also a moral, social, ideological and sexual exile."*
Juan Goytisolo

SIREN

Same as it ever was
Same as it ever was
History draws its substance
from the Archives of Blood
We are all gravediggers to the future
Each generation raises monuments
To the executioners which have preceded it
Society is not a disease it's a fucking disaster

History has been reduced to thousands of snapshots rifled
through the air like a broken film strip ripped through an
ancient projector and I don't know about you but my mind works
in multiples tripping over images which beg for deliverance from
the place that time smolders

Blind spots: Blackouts: Vertigo: Limbo

Flashbacks of great disasters
Frozen moments in time unfold

The Spanish Inquisition, 400 years of the Crusades, Joan of Arc,
The Fall of the Bastille, The Black Plague, Pompeii, Babylon,
Bhopal, Chernobyl, Hiroshima, Three Mile Island, World War
One, World War Two, World War Three, The Korean War, The
Vietnam War, The Gulf War, Bosnia Herzegovina, Iraq, Iran,
Afghanistan, The World Trade Centers...

Replay over and over again
Manmade catastrophes
Which have impregnated
Our psychic fabric

Are we all suffering from collective induced
fiction, an ambushed memory—
the unwitting victims of a historical lobotomy
all stuck wallowing in Orwell's Memory Hole?

191

My memory is always running backwards
Toward the vault of eternity
That black pyramid of death
Whose accumulated catastrophes just keep billowing on
Forever and ever toward the edge of the Earth

Oh Earth Planet of Birth and Death
Release me from this Menace of Memory
From this psychological lockjaw
Where life is just a thief it steals everything
Creation is but a nightmare spectacle
We are all just trembling accidents
Germinating here on this hot house planet
Which has been soaked with the blood of all its creatures
For hundreds of thousands of years now
Same as it ever was
Same as it ever was

193

EMPTY ARMS   *WHAT ONCE WAS*

CONDEMNED

STILL LIFE

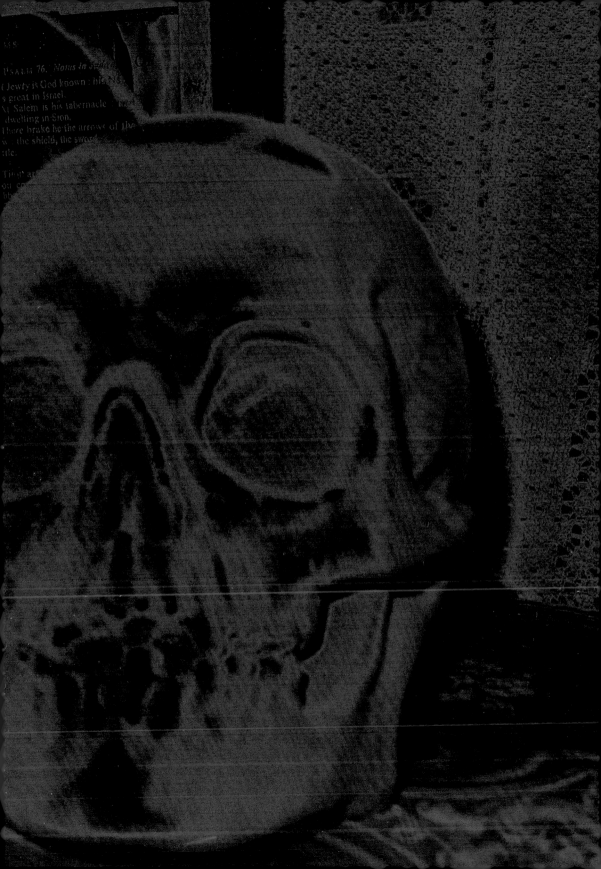

I'LL PRAY FOR YOU

This is for the ghosts
This is for the ghosts of
Guernica, Belchite, Badajoz
El Mazuco, Jarama, Monte Pelato
Cape Palos, Mataró.

This is for the dead and dying.

This is for the war torn and battle fatigued
For the widows and orphans of warriors
This is for the warriors
Who were willing to die for their beliefs
Who were willing to die
Because they believed it is better to die
Fighting for freedom
Than to live a life enslaved by lies.

This is for those who believe.

And you better believe
You better believe in ghosts
Because soon enough you too will become one.

This is for the ghosts of Fallujah, Anbar Provence, Abu Ghraib, Baquba,
Guantanamo, Gaza, Beirut, Bagdad, Kabul, Kandahar, Jalalabad, Islamabad,
Katmandu, Mogadishu, Darfur, Sierra Leone.

This is for the freedom fighters, the insurgents, the rebels and the rabble rousers
and for every individual
who revolts against tyranny and oppression.

This is for the martyrs—
Mohammed Mossadeq, Salvador Allende, Óscar Romero,
Theo Van Gogh, Federico García Lorca, Pasolini, Bruno Schulz,
Madalyn Murray O'Hair.

This is for my ghost—
For the twin who did not survive his first breath
Who gave his life so I might live to write these words
Never allowing me to forget just how close we all are to death
That all consuming inevitable, the master thief who steals everything.
Reminding me everyday to make every moment count.
And to never stop fighting for what I believe in.
To never stop fighting. To never stop.
To never give up the ghost.

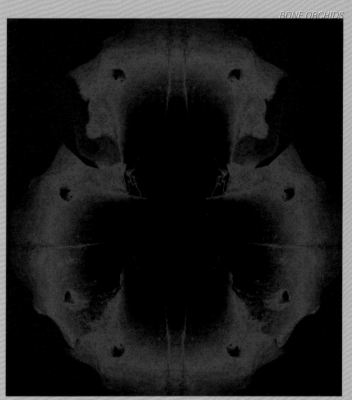
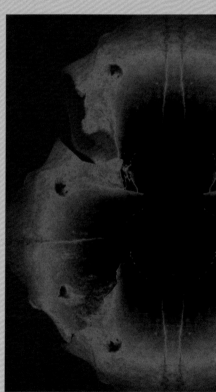

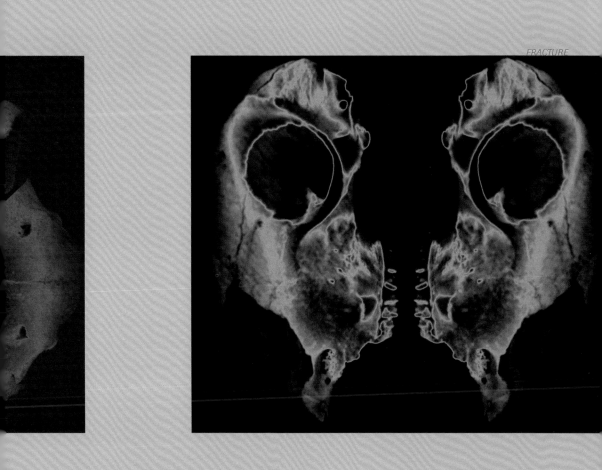

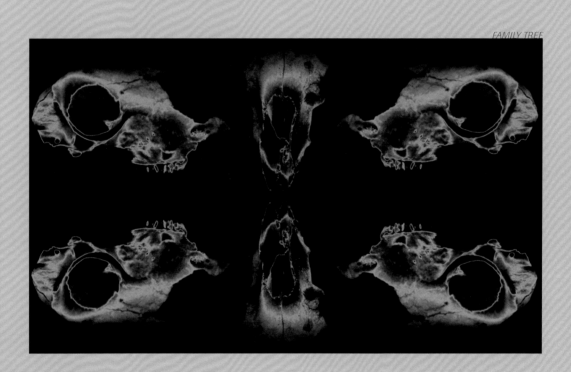

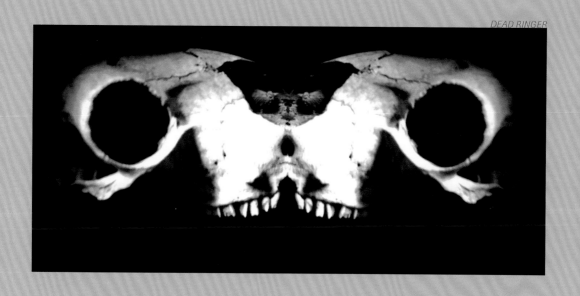

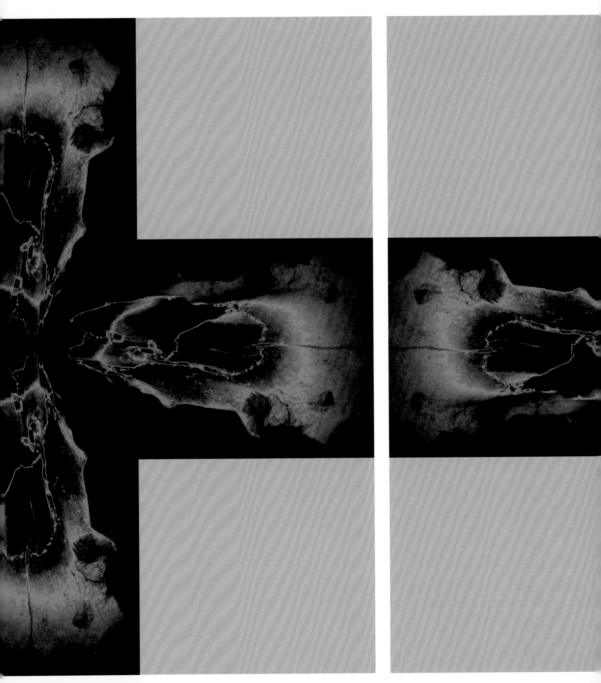

215

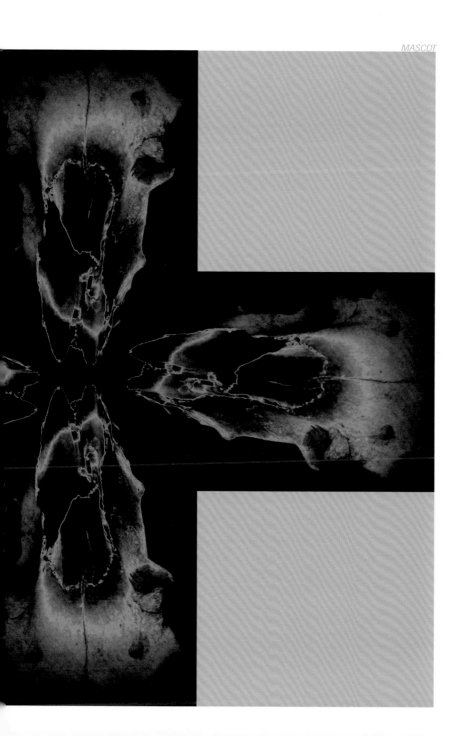

UP FROM THE ASHES

MEMORIAL

I AM AN ISLAND IN THIS CESSPOOL CALLED HISTORY
I INHABIT THE CRUMPLED REMAINS
OF A PLACE THAT ONCE WAS...
SUFFOCATING IN A SOLITUDE SO FULFILLING
THAT THE MEREST RENDEZVOUS
BECOMES A CRUCIFIXION

A SOLITUDE MORE CHAOTIC THAN WAR
A STOIC WHO REMAINS UNDAUNTED AMONG THE RUINS
OF A WORLD SHATTERED INTO ATOMS
SOME OF US ARE BORNE WEARY OF BEING BORN
WE ARE GIVEN THE GIFT OF LIFE
TO LIVE OBSESSED WITH DEATH

WE BURY ON OUR SOULS THE CORPSES
WE HAVE NOT YET MURDERED...
LIKE AN ANGEL DRAFTED ON TO THE
BACK OF A LEPER...
A CRIMINAL SAINT...
THE HERO OF YESTERDAY
BECOMES THE TYRANT OF TOMORROW
UNLESS HE CRUCIFIES HIMSELF TODAY....

THE RESTLESSNESS OF SLEEPLESS NIGHTS DIG TRENCHES
WHERE THE CORPSES OF MEMORY LAY ROTTING...
A CRATER OF LUCIDITY WHISPERS... TIME... TIME...
THAT SLAUGHTER HOUSE OF THE UNIVERSE...
WHERE IS IT NOT IN THE NATURE OF A MAN WHO
CANNOT KILL HIMSELF TO SEEK REVENGE AGAINST
WHATEVER ENJOYS EXISTING

A song stolen from, inspired by and returned to EM Cioran

RETROSPECTIVE
OF WORKS

COLLABORATIONS, COMPILATIONS, SOLO RELEASES AND GUEST APPEARANCES

1978	*No New York (Compilation)*
1978	*Orphans/Less of Me*
1979	*Beirut Slump*
1979	*Off White James White and the Blacks*
1979	*Baby Doll/Freud in Flop/Race Mixing*
1979	*Pink 12" EP*
1979	*Pre-Teenage Jesus & The Jerks*
1980	*8-Eyed Spy*
1980	*Queen Of Siam*
1981	*8-Eyed Spy*
1981	*8-Eyed Spy Live*
1981	*Diddy Wah Diddy*
1982	*1313*
1982	*Some Velvet Morning w/Rowland S Howard*
1982	*The Agony Is The Ecstacy*
1982	*Thirsty Animal Einstürzende Neubauten*
1982	*Vortex—Original Soundtrack*
1982	*Der Karibische Western Die Haut*
1983	*Dagger & Guitar Sort Sol*
1983	*The Last Testament*
1984	*Better A New Demon Than An Old God (Compilation)*
1984	*Plow! (Compilation)*
1984	*In Limbo w/Thurston Moore*
1984	*Speed Trials (Compilation)*
1984	*Death Valley '69 7in w/Sonic Youth*
1984	*Hard Rock*
1985	*The Uncensored Lydia Lunch*
1985	*Heart Of Darkness No Trend*
1985	*The Drowning Of Lucy Hamilton*
1985	*A Dozen of Dead Roses No Trend*
1985	*Tellus The Audio Cassette Magazine #10: All Guitars!*
1986	*Hysterie (Compilation)*
1987	*Tellus, The Audio Cassette Magazine #18: Experimental Theater*
1988	*Honeymoon In Red w/Rowland S Howard*
1988	*Oral Fixation*
1988	*Stinkfist w/Clint Ruin*
1988	*The Crumb w/Clint Ruin and Thurston Moore*
1989	*Fear, Power, God (Compilation)*
1989	*New York Rockers (Manhattan's Original Rock Underground)*
1989	*Zetrospective, Vol. I: Dancing in the Face of Adversity*
1990	*Conspiracy Of Women (COW)*
1990	*Our Fathers Who Aren't In Heaven*
1990	*Naked In Garden Hills Harry Crews*
1990	*Stinkfist & The Crumb (Re-issue)*
1990	*A Girl Doesn't Get Killed by a Make Believe Lover/Cuz it's Hot Thrill Kill Kultt*
1991	*Trying To Make It To The End Of The Century*
1991	*Don't Fear The Reaper w/Clint Ruin*
1991	*POW*
1991	*Shotgun Wedding w/Rowland S Howard*
1991	*Queen of Siam (Re-issue)*
1991	*King of the Jews Oxbow*
1992	*Head On Die Haut*
1992	*Downtown Does The Beatles*
1993	*Sweat Die Haut*
1993	*Shotgun Wedding Live*
1993	*Unearthly Delights*
1993	*Queen of Siam (Re-issue)*
1993	*Welcome to My Nightmare (Tribute to Alice Cooper)*
1993	*Fear Engine II: Almost As If It Never Happened*
1993	*13 Above the Night Thrill Kill Kult*
1993	*Workdogs In Hell (Compilation)*
1994	*Crimes Against Nature*
1994	*Transmutation & Shotgun Wedding Live*
1995	*Teenage Jesus & The Jerks—Everything*
1995	*The Drowning Of Lucy Hamilton/In Limbo*
1995	*Rude Hieroglyphics w/Exene Cervenka*
1995	*Arkkon David Knight*
1996	*Uncensored/Oral Fixation (Re-issue)*
1996	*Universal Infiltrators w/David Knight*

1978 *NO NEW YORK*

1978 *ORPHANS/LESS OF ME*

1979 *BABY DOLL*

1979 *PRE-TEENAGE JESUS & THE JERKS*

1980 *QUEEN OF SIAM*

1980 *QUEEN OF SIAM*

1981 *8-EYED SPY*

1981 *8-EYED SPY*

1982 *1313*

1982 *SOME VELVET MORNING W/ ROWLAND S HOWARD*

1982 *THE AGONY IS THE ECSTASY*

1982 *VORTEX—ORIGINAL SOUNDTRACK*

1988 *HONEYMOON IN RED*

1988 *ORAL FIXATION*

1990 *CONSPIRACY OF WOMAN (COW)*

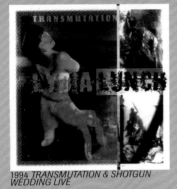
1994 *TRANSMUTATION & SHOTGUN WEDDING LIVE*

1995 *RUDE HIEROGLYPHICS*

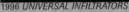
1996 *UNIVERSAL INFILTRATORS*

1996 *STINKFIST*

1998 *MATRIKAMANTRA*

1998 *WIDOWSPEAK*

1999 *THE BLAIR WITCH PROJECT/ ORIGINAL SOUNDTRACK*

1999 *SHOTGUN WEDDING LIVE*

1996	Home Alive (Compilation)	1998	Crippled Champions: The Soundtrack Generation
1996	Flesh, Fangs & Filigree (Compilation): "Stinkfist"	1999	Radio History of KBUR FM (Compilation), reading rom "Paradoxia"
1996	Flesheaters (Compilation): "In My Time of Dying"	1999	Crimes Against Nature (Re-issue)
1996	Undead (Compilation): "Twisted" and "Some Velvet Morning"	1999	Original Soundtrack: The Blair Witch Project
1996	No Excuse w/Lee Renaldo	1999	Shotgun Wedding Live w/Rowland S Howard
1996	Out of Their Mouths, MK 2 An Atavistic Compilation	1999	Terry Edwards Yesterday's Zeitgeist
		1999	Dirty Little Secrets—Music to Strip By... Thrill Kill Kult
1996	Mind the Gap Vol. 9	1999	Re-Up Étant Donnés
1997	Kiss of the Vampire (Compilation): "Stinkfist" and "Some Velvet Morning"	1999	Drinking from Puddles
1997	Necromantic (Compilation): "In My Time of Dying"	1999	Education In Infestation
		1999	Kaleidoscope 6
1997	KEROUAC: Kick Joy Darkness Tribute to Jack Kerouac Compilation	2000	New Coat of Paint
		2000	Rotunda
1997	8-Eyed Spy: "Luncheone"	2000	Terry Edwards Ontogeny—No Fish Is Too Weird For Her Aquarium
1997	The Desperate Ones w/Glyn Styler	2000	The Devil's Racetrack
1997	York The Foetus Symphony Orchestra	2000	Beauty and Terror
1997	Grrrl Power: A History of Women in Popular Music: "Some Velvet Morning"	2001	Hangover Hotel
		2001	Downtown '81 (Original Soundtrack)
1997	Stiletto Vamp (Compilation): "Burning Skulls"	2002	Champagne, Cocaine & Nicotine Stains w/Anubians Lights
1997	Vital Juices	2002	Blue Light Fever
1997	Dead & Gone #2: Totenlieder	2002	"&" Kristian Hoffman
1998	Here: Brooklyn Bank	2002	Wake The Dead: Words & Music from Sex and Guts
1998	Gothic Erotica (Compilation): "Stinkfist" and "Burning Skulls"	2002	The Sound of Il Giaguaro Vol. 2
1998	Before the Balloon Went Up (Compilation): "In My Time of Dying"	2002	Electric Jazz Vol. 1
		2002	Nu Jazz Vol. 3
1998	Uturn/Minox	2003	In Our Time of Dying
1998	Matrikamantra	2003	Memory and Madness
1998	Queen of Siam (Re-issue)	2003	Exploding Plastic Pleasure
1998	Songs of the Witchblade (Compilation)	2003	Terry Edwards Queer Street No Fish Is Too Weird for Her Acquarium Vol. III
1998	Widowspeak (Greatest Hits Compilation)		
1998	Honeymoon In Red w/Rowland S Howard	2004	Smoke In The Shadows
1998	Il Juke Box Del DiAvolo	2004	Live in London DVD

2000 *NEW COAT OF PAINT*

2000 *THE DEVIL'S RACETRACK*

2001 *HANGOVER HOTEL*

2002 *CHAMPAGNE, COCAINE & NICOTINE STAINS*

2003 *IN OUR TIME OF DYING*

2004 *SMOKE IN THE SHADOWS*

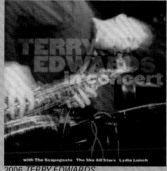

2006 *TERRY EDWARDS SARTORIAL SAMPLER*

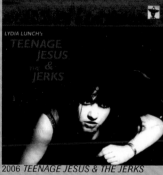

2006 *TEENAGE JESUS & THE JERKS*

2006 *DEVIATIONS ON A THEME*

2008 *GHOSTS OF SPAIN*

EXHIBITIONS

Nov 2006	Ecstasy at the Mouth of the Abyss, Galerie Kennory Kim, Paris, France.
May 2004	The Scene Of The Crime Could Be Anywhere At Anytime, exhibition with Marc Viaplana.
	You Are Not Safe in Your Own Home, installation.
	FIERCE Festival, Birmingham, England.
Sept 1998	Gallery Luscombe, San Francisco, CA, mixed media.
	La Luz De Jesus, Los Angeles, CA, mixed media.
July 1998	Zenith Gallery, Pittsburgh, PA, mixed media.
May 1998	La Musardine, Paris, France, photography.
March 1998	Gandy Gallery, Prague, Czech Republic, photography.
Nov 1997	Tribal Act, Paris, France, photography.
	Pez-Ner, Lyon, France, photography.
	Effenar, Eindhoven, Holland, photography.
Oct 1997	New Image Art Gallery, Los Angeles, CA, photography.
June 1997	Harold & Maude's, Orlando, FL, photography.
May 1997	2 South Gallery, Detroit, MI, photography.
Oct 1995	Rita Dean Gallery, San Diego, CA, photography.

LYDIA

LUNCH

jeudi 26 octobre

Soirée Lydia Lunch

projection de films, de documents
rares, musique, lectures ...
à partir de 20h30

...

La Cantada
13 rue Moret
750011 Paris
www.cantada.fr

Rencontre-Signature

de 19h à 20h30 au vidéoclub-librairie
Hors-circuits autour de deux ouvrages:
"Paradoxia, journal d'une prédatrice" et
"Aussi haut que nous le pourrons" ainsi que
des CD et DVD produits par Lydia Lunch

...

Hors-circuits
4 rue de Nemours
75011 Paris
www.horscircuits.com

jeudi 2 novembre

1er novembre . 9 décembre 2006

EXPOSITION

"Ecstasy at the Mouth of the Abyss"

photographies, installations sonores et vidéo ... by Lydia Lunch

galerie kennory kim

22 rue des Vertus 75003 Paris - mar/sam - 14h/20h30
www.kennory-kim.com ... info@kennory-kim.com

Plus d'infos sur la semaine Lydia Lunch sur le site de notre partenaire Hors-circuits

PLAYS

1990   *Smell of Guilt*, by Lydia Lunch and Emilio Cubeiro. Written,
        performed, directed and produced with Emilio Cubeiro, Dance
        Theatre Workshop 10th anniversary, New York.
1988   *South of Your Border*, by Lydia Lunch and Emilio Cubeiro. Written,
        performed, directed and produced with Emilio Cubeiro. New
        Theatre, New York.

LEFT AND RIGHT: SCENES FROM SOUTH
OF YOUR BORDER, *1988.*
OPPOSITE: POSTER FOR SOUTH OF
YOUR BORDER, *1988.*

INTERNATIONAL THEATRE OF POETRY AND PAIN PRODUCTION

NEW YORK SPOT

SOUTH OF YOUR BORDER

SETS: Richard Phillips
LIGHTS: David Adams
MUSIC: J.G. Thirlwell
GRAPHICS: Mark O

Wednesdays-Sundays 8pm Jan. 6-17 1988   THE NEW THEATER   62 East 4th Street

TICKETS $13

LYDIA LUNCH · EMILIO CUBEIRO

NIGHTMARE
South
Of Your
Border

A play in six scenes: An experimental exploration into the cause and effect of the many faces of oppression. Your worst nightmare has finally come true!

SICK SEX SCANDAL

An uptight anally retentive member of the United States Military Intelligence Service singles YOU out for an in-depth detailed investigation...Ultimately culminating in a life sentence on death row. But, not before they have dissected what they consider to be the many symptoms of YOUR HABITUAL OBSESSIONS, DEVIATIONS AND DISEASES, which due to the nature of what they term your INSANITY, you are forced to live out again...and again...and again...

RATED XXX

2007	*Lydia Lunch/Real Pornography* (documentary on the artist), directed by Ludovic Cantais, La Luna Films.
	Llik Your Idols, directed by Angelique Bosio.
	Santa Cruz County Anti-Meth Campaign PSA (narrator), directed by Cam Archer.
2006	*Kill Your Idols* (interview), directed by Scott A Crary.
2005	*American Fame Pt. 2: Forgetting Jonathan Brandis* (narrator), directed by Cam Archer.
2004	*American Fame Pt. 1: The Drowning of River Phoenix* (narrator), directed by Cam Archer.
	The Heart Is Deceitful Above All Things (cameo appearance, photography), directed by Asia Argento.
2002	*D.I.Y. OR DIE* (interview), directed by Michael W Dean.
2000	*Shadow Hours* (scene writer, consultant), directed by Isaac H Eaton.
1997	*Girls Girls Girls* (performed), directed by Ellen Maki.
1996	*Visiting Desire* (acted), directed by Beth B.
1995	*The Power of the Word* (appearance), directed by Jeanne Harco.
1992	*Malicious Intent* (spoken word, performance), directed by Richard Kern and Chris Lovenko.
	The Thunder, The Perfect Mind (acted, narrator), directed by Tom Richards Murphy and Marta Ze.
1990	*BBQ Death Squad* (acted), directed by Penn and Teller.
	Kiss Napoleon Goodbye (acted, wrote, co-directed), directed by Babeth and Lydia Lunch.
	Thanatopsis (acted, wrote), directed by Beth B.
	The Road To God Knows Where, Nick Cave and the Bad Seeds documentary (cameo appearance).
1988	*The Gun Is Loaded* (acted, wrote), directed by Merill Aldighieri and Joe Tripician.
1987	*Submit To Me Now* (acted), directed by Richard Kern.
	Put More Blood Into The Music (interview).
	Mondo New York (appearance), directed by Harvey Keith.
1986	*Fingered* (acted, wrote), directed by Richard Kern.
	The Invisible Thread (acted), directed by Penn and Teller.
	Gang of Souls, spoken word documentary by Maria Beatty.
1985	*Submit To Me* (acted), directed by Richard Kern.
1984	*The Right Side of My Brain* (acted, wrote), directed by Richard Kern.
1983	MTV's *The Cutting Edge* (appeared in six episodes).
	Vortex (acted), directed by Beth and Scott B.
	Like Dawn To Dust (acted), directed by Vivienne Dick.
1980	*Liberty's Booty*, directed by Vivienne Dick.
	The Offenders (acted), directed by Beth and Scott B.
1979	*Beauty Becomes The Beast* (acted), directed by Vivienne Dick.
	Alien Portrait (appeared in performance), directed by Michael McClard.
1978	*Guerillere Talks* (acted), directed by Vivienne Dick.
	Black Box (acted), directed by Beth and Scott B.
	She Had Her Gun All Ready (acted), directed by Vivienne Dick.
	Rome '78 (acted), directed by James Nares.

POSTER FOR BLACK BOX, *1978.*

LYDIA LUNCH   BOB MASON

BLACK BOX

A FILM BY BETH B & SCOTT B ©1978

3 october 1996 to
5 january 1997

no wave cinema
1978-87

FOR SCREENING INFORMATION: (212) 570 3676

whitney museum of american art
945 madison avenue @ 75th street

the whitney. where american art lives

POSTER FOR THE NO WAVE CINEMA
SEASON AT WHITNEY MUSEUM OF
AMERICAN ART, 1986–1987.

BIBLIOGRAPHY

2008   *Paradoxia: A Predator's Diary* (introduction by Virginie Despentes and Thurston Moore),
        Spanish translation published by Melusina Books.

2007   *Paradoxia: A Predator's Diary* (introduction by Jerry Stahl and Thurston Moore),
        published by Akashic Books.

2003   *Sex and Guts* (written and edited with Gene Gregorits), published by Phony Ltd Books.

1999   *Lady Lazarus* (written by Maren Hancunt), published by Questing Beast Ltd.

1998   *Toxic Gumbo* (art by Ted McKeever), published by DC Comics/Vertigo Press.

1997   *Paradoxia: A Predator's Diary* (introduction by Hubert Selby Jr),
        published by Creation Press. French edition by La Musardine, 1998; Czech by Mata,1999;
        German by Miranda Verlag, 2000; Spanish Edition, 2000; Russian edition by
        Adaptec/T-ough Press, 003; Italian edition by Storie Press, 2005.

1993   *As.fix.e.8* (with Nick Cave, illustrated by Mike Matthews), published by Last Gasp.

1992   *Incriminating Evidence* (illustrations by Kristian Hoffman), published by Last Gasp.
        Blood Sucker (illustrated by Bob Fingerman), published by Fantagraphics/Eros Press.

1987   *The Right Side of My Brain* (limited edition printing with erotic drawings by
        Knut Odde, Denmark).

1982   *Adulterers Anonymous* (poetry collaboration with Exene Cervenka), published by Grove
        Press, re-issued in 1996 by Last Gasp

CLOCKWISE FROM TOP LEFT:
FRONT COVERS FOR ADULTERERS
ANONYMOUS, *1982,* BLOOD SUCKER,
1992, INCRIMINATING EVIDENCE, *1992,*
AND TOXIC GUMBO, *1998.*

OVERLEAF (CLOCKWISE FROM LEFT):
FRONT COVERS FOR LADY LAZARUS,
1999, PARADOXIA: A PREDATOR'S
DIARY, *VARIOUS EDITIONS.*

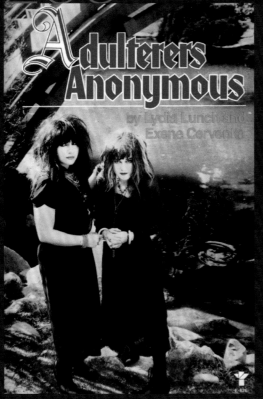

ADULTERERS ANONYMOUS

by Lydia Lunch and Exene Cervenka

E-826

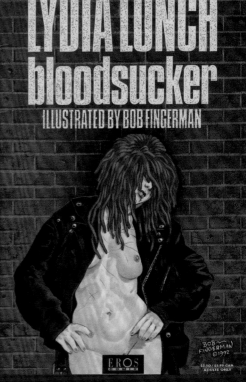

LYDIA LUNCH
bloodsucker
ILLUSTRATED BY BOB FINGERMAN

BOB FINGERMAN ©1992

EROS COMIX

$3.50/$3.95 CAN
ADULTS ONLY

Lydia Lunch

INCRIMINATING EVIDENCE

Illustrated by Kristian Hoffman

LAST GASP

DC COMICS VERTIGO

TOXIC GUMBO

Lydia Lunch
Ted McKeever

LADY LAZARUS

CONFRONTING LYDIA LUNCH
MAREN HANCUNT
INTRODUCTION BY JESSICA LAWLESS
CONTAINS TWO EXTENSIVE INTERVIEWS WITH LYDIA LUNCH

237

PARADOXIA
A PREDATOR'S DIARY

Lunch

Lydia

LYDIA LUNCH

Introduction by Hubert Selby Jr.

Paradoxia

LYDIA LUNCH
PARADOXIE

TAGEBUCH EINES RAUBTIERS

MIT EINEM VORWORT VON HUBERT SELBY JR.

mirandA-Verlag

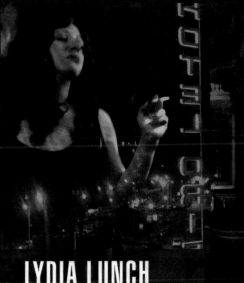

**LYDIA LUNCH
PARADOXIA
A PREDATOR'S DIARY**

INTRODUCTION BY **JERRY STAHL**
AFTERWORD BY **THURSTON MOORE**

SELECTED ARTICLES AND WRITINGS

2008	"Introduction", *NO WAVE: Post Punk Underground New York 1976–1980*, Thurston Moore and Byron Coley eds., published by Abrams Image.
	"The Spirit of Philosophical Vitriol", *Istanbul Noir*, published by Akashic Books.
	"Illusive Bitch", *Awake: A Reader for the Sleepless*, published by Soft Skull Press.
2007	"Johnny Behind the Deuce" and "Real Pornography", *One On One: The Best Women's Monologues for the Twenty-First Century*, published by Applause Books.
2005	"Johnny Behind the Deuce", published by Storie Leconte.
2004	*Sin-A-Rama: Sleaze Sex Paperbacks of the Sixties*, Lydia Lunch ed., published by Feral House.
	"Women and Children First", *50 Reason NOT to Vote for Bush*, published by Feral House Press.
2002	"Motherhood is Not Compulsory", *Inappropriate Behaviour*, published by Serpent's Tail Press.
1999	"Tough Love" (weekly website column), *Getting It* magazine.
	"Original Beat/Herbert Huncke", *Rolling Stone Book of Beats*, published by Rolling Stone Press.
	Excerpt from novel *Paradoxia*, *Pure Magazine*, Vol. 1.
1998	Excerpt from novel *Paradoxia*, *Hustler Magazine*.
1997	Introduction in "Visions Sublime", *Juxtapoz Erotica*, October issue.
	"Introduction", *New York Girls*, published by Taschen Publishing.
	Essay on multi-media artist, Jane Handel, *Juxtapoz*, May issue.
	Petty Intrusion (short story), *Noirotica II: Pulp Friction*, published by Rhinoceros Press.
1996–1998	Ongoing contributor, *World Arts Magazine*.
1995	"Introduction", *JK Potter's Neurotica*, published by Tiger Press.
	"Introduction", *Metropol*, published by Blue Eyed Dog Press.
1993	"Cruel Story of Youth", *The Girl Wants To*, published by Coach House Press.
1989	"Introduction",*Visual Addiction*, Robert Williams ed., published by Last Gasp.
1986	Vampire's Kiss (short story), published by Penthouse Forum.
1985	Text from film Right Side of My Brain, published by Penthouse Forum.
1984	Interview with Pat Benetar, *Spin Magazine*.

FRONT COVER OF FORCED EXPOSURE FEATURING INTERVIEW WITH LYDIA LUNCH, 1986.

#10 $2.50

FORCED EXPOSURE

LYDIA LUNCH:
THE INTERVIEW

Also:

**Gary
Panter**

**Meatmen
Tour
Diary**

**Die
Kreuzen**

Angst

**Worst
of '85
Poll Results**

**And
MORE**

PORTRAITS 1970s

240

© RESNICK

© GEORGE DUBOSE

© JULIE GORTON

RETROSPECTIVE OF WORKS

© GEORGE DUBOSE

© MARCY BLAUSTEIN

© BIRRER

© ED CULVER

© MARCY BLAUSTEIN

© MICHAEL LAVINE

© DAVID ARNOFF

© MICHAEL KENNEDY

© MARCUS LEATHERDALE

© BIRRER

© KEN WINOKUR W/EXENE CERVENKA

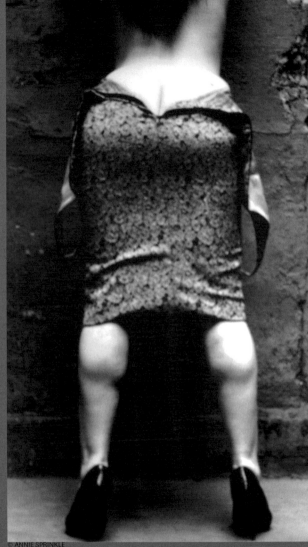

© ANNIE SPRINKLE

© BART D. FRESCURA

247

© JK POTTER

© BART D. FRESCURA

© DORALBO PICERNO

© W ROWLAND S. HOWARD

© DAVE NAZ

© DAVE NAZ

© MARC VIAPLANA

© TOM GARRETSON

© MARC VIAPLANA

CREDITS

MONONGAHELA/Pittsburgh, Pennsylvania, 1995-1996

Dead River

Fall

Southside

Squirrel Hill

Mckees Rock

Storm Warning

First Date

Mr Fix It

Last Call

First Date

The Price you Pay

Last to Arrive

ALL MY HEROES ARE KILLERS

Adam, New Orleans, Louisiana, 1991

Adam and Alejandro, New Orleans, Louisiana, 1991

Leo, Pittsburgh, Pennsylvania, 1995

Rusty, Pittsburgh, Pennsylvania, 1995

Dylan, Knoxville, Tennessee, 2003

Dylan, Knoxville, Tennessee, 2003

Dylan, Knoxville, Tennessee, 2003

Eddy, New Orleans, Louisiana, 1991

Jonah, New Orleans, Louisiana, 1992

Johnny, Knoxville, Tennessee, 2003

Adam, New Orleans, Louisiana, 1991

Jimmy, Knoxville, Tennessee, 2003

FATAL BEAUTY

Gene Gregorits, Los Angeles California 2000

Litmus Test

Bad Mood Rising 1, 2

When Words Fail

If I Could Only Piece You Back Together

You Broke My Fucking Heart

THE DEATH OF INNOCENCE

You Made Me, Cole, Knoxville, Tennessee, 2003, Construction Site, Barcelona, 2007

Ghostgirl, Ava June Hazelmyer, Minneapolis, Minnesota, 2003

Dissolution Angels, Jimmy, John, Aaron, Tommy, Knoxville, Tennessee, 2003, Construction Site, Barcelona, Spain, 2007

Little Luger, Ava June Hazelmyer, Minneapolis, Minnesota, 2003, Construction Site, Barcelona, 2007

The Death of Innocence, Dylan, Knoxville, Tennessee, 2003, Fire Bombing, Chicago, 2004

He'll Grow Out of It, Leo Kramer, Pittsburgh, Pennsylvannia, 1995

Sleepwalker, Ava June Hazelmyer, Minneapolis, Minnesota, 2003, Original Landscape Photograph, Jacob Kirkegaard, Chernobyl, 2005

Retribution, Dylan, Knoxville, Tennessee, 2003, Firebombed Photograph, Studio Chattanooga, Tennessee, 2003

Daddy Loves You, Jimmy and Ben Foster, Knoxville, Tennessee, 2003, Woods, Minneapolis, Minnesota, 2005

Teenage Wasteland, Milkshake, Truckstop, Knoxville, Tennessee, 2003

Detention, Johnavah, New Orleans, Louisiana, 1991, Junked Truck, Pittsburgh, Pennsylvania, 1996

Breakout, Johnavah, New Orleans, Louisiana 1991, Original Landscape Photograph, Jacob Kirkegaard, Chernobyl, 2005

HIEROMANCY/self portraits 2002–2007

Third Eye, Fire Bombed Building, Chicago, Illinois, 2004

Elemental, Abandoned Building, Poblo Nou, Barcelona, Spain, 2006

Rehabitual, Abandoned Psychiatric Hospital, Knoxville, Tennessee, 2003

Chemical Imbalance, Meth Lab, Knoxville, Tennessee, 2003

Fever Dreams, Kutna Hora Bone House, Czech Republic, 1998

Vaudouisant, Junkyard, Knoxville, Tennessee, 2003

Pawn Breaker, Firebombed Photographic Studio, Knoxville, Tennessee, 2003

SPECTROPHILIA/self portraits 2002–2007

Casita Blanca, Whorehouse, Barcelona, Spain, 2003, Devonshire House, Birmingham, UK, 2002

Bliss, Abandoned Building, Bari, Italy, 2006

The Promise of Paradise, Belchite, Spain, 2004

Alchemical, Poblo Nou, Barcelona, Spain, 2007

Prophesy, Abattoir, Ljubljana, Slovenia, 2007

Pray to God, Belchite, Spain, 2004

Baby's on Fire, Firebombed Photographic Studio, Knoxville, Tennessee, 2003

Rubidium, Firebombed Photographic Studio, Knoxville, Tennessee, 2003

Inside Out, Church, Chernobyl, Original Landscape Photograph, Jacob Kirkegaard, 2005

INSOMNIAC THEATRE/self portraits 2002–2007

Try Me, Devonshire House, Birmingham, UK, 2002

The Scent of a Ghost, Devonshire House

Lead Poisoning, Barcelona, Spain, 2006

Streetsweeper, New York City, 2007

Killer Urge, Barcelona, Spain, 2006

Luminal, Barcelona, Spain, 2006

Disappearance, Barcelona, Spain, 2006

THE SICKNESS OF STRANGERS

Bobby Knows, Emilio Cubeiro, Found Photograph 1982, Devonshire House, Birmingham, UK, 2002

Beyond Flesh and Blood, Pierce and Massimo 2004, Junkyard, Knoxville, Tennessee, 2003, Original Portrait by Raffaele Buccomino
Prison of Memories, Gene Gregorits, Carmi Paulson, Glendale, California, 2001, Construction Site, Barcelona, 2007
Hellhouse, Asia Argento and Jeremy Sisto, Knoxville, Tennessee, 2003
Psychic Surgery, Ben Foster 2003, Abandoned Psychiatric Hospital, Knoxville, Tennessee, 2003

SHADOWHOURS

Transduction, Jade, Los Angeles, California, 2000
The Guardian, Daryl Carlton, Los Angeles, California, 2000
Trance, Jade, Los Angeles, California, 2000
Beyond the Grave, Kelly and Clayton, Los Angeles, California, 2001
Penetraitor, Kelly and Clayton, Los Angeles, California, 2001
Internal Combustion, Cyril, Los Angeles, California, 2001
Crystalized, Kelly and Clayton, Los Angeles, California, 2001
More Than You Know, Cyril and Karen, Los Angeles, California, 2001
In the Zone, Paul and Claudio, Los Angeles, California, 2001

THE SCENE OF THE CRIME COULD BE ANYWHERE AT ANY TIME/Collaboration with Marc Viaplana, Barcelona, Los Angeles and Chicago, 2003

Bottom Floor
Heatseeker
Mac 10
Wanted in Connection
Composite
Full Auto, Original Portrait by Marcy Blaustein, 1981
Recoil
Upload
Evidence
Endgame
Flee

ARCHITECT OF DESIRE

Something in the Water, Barcelona, 2007
Sweat Factory, Barcelona, 2007
Two in the Chamber, Barcelona, 2007
Recipe for Disaster, Barcelona, 2007
Still Life, Barcelona, 2007
Abattoir, Ljubljana, Slovenia, 2007
Macumba, Barcelona, 2007
Your Ghost Stinks Up Everything, Original Sculpture by Paul Toupet, Landscape, Ljubljana, Slovenia, 2007
What Falls through the Cracks, Morgue, Barcelona, 2007

LANDSCAPES AFTER THE BATTLE/Belchite, Spain, 2005

Siren
Battle Fatigue
A Bruise in Time
The Bones of Things
Empty Arms
Where Once Was
Devout
Cruel Beauty
Condemned

STILL LIFE

Solitude, Metarie Cemetery, New Orleans, Louisiana, 1991
Last Words, Allegheny Cemetery, Pittsburgh, Pennsylvania, 1995
Milova, Vysehrad Cemetery, Prague, Czech Republic, 1997
Gifted, Brno, Czech Republic, 1997
I'll Pray For You, Pére-Lachaise Cemetery, Paris, France, 1997
Motherlove, Vysehrad Cemetery, Prague, Czech Republic, 1997
From the East, Vysehrad Cemetery, Prague, Czech Republic, 1997
Soldier On, Vysehrad Cemetery, Prague, Czech Republic, 1997
Bone Orchids, Coyote Skull, 2007
Fracture, Coyote Skull, 2007
Family Tree, Coyote Skull, 2007
Dead Ringer, Coyote Skull, 2007
Mascot, Coyote Skull, 2007
Up From the Ashes, Collaboration with Marc Viaplana

ACKNOWLEDGEMENTS

Thanks to Jack Sargeant, Marc Viaplana, Tom Garretson,
JK Potter, R Kern, JG Thirlwell, Marcy Blaustein, Jacob
Kirkegaard, Cathi Unsworth, and Black Sun Productions.

Inspired by EM Cioran, Juan Goytisolo, Karl Heinzen,
Madalyn Murray O'Hair, Pier Paolo Pasolini, Henry Miller,
Hubert Selby, Jr, Samuel Fuller, Elia Kazan, Emma Goldman,
Ulrike Meinhof, Unica Zürn, Hans Bellmar and
Marcel Duchamp.

Edited by Blanche Craig at Black Dog Publishing.
Designed by Julia Trudeau Rivest at Black Dog Publishing.

Black Dog Publishing Limited
10A Acton Street
London WC1X 9NG
United Kingdom

Tel: +44 (0) 20 7713 5097
Fax: +44 (0) 20 7713 8682
info@blackdogonline.com
www.blackdogonline.com

British Library Cataloguing-in-Publication Data.

A CIP record for this book is available from the
British Library.

ISBN: 978 1 906155 30 8

Black Dog Publishing Limited, London, UK, is an
environmentally responsible company. *The Gun is Loaded* is
printed on Sappi Magno Satin, a chlorine-free paper,
FSC certified.

architecture art design
fashion history photography
theory and things

black dog
publishing

london uk